Doomed!

THE SINKING OF THE TITANIC

By Therese Shea

Gareth Stevens
PUBLISHING

Please visit our website, www.garethstevens.com. For a free color catalog
of all our high-quality books, call toll free 1-800-542-2595 or fax 1-877-542-2596.

Library of Congress Cataloging-in-Publication Data

Shea, Therese.
 The sinking of the Titanic / Therese Shea.
    pages cm — (Doomed!)
 Includes bibliographical references and index.
 ISBN 978-1-4824-2944-2 (pbk.)
 ISBN 978-1-4824-2945-9 (6 pack)
 ISBN 978-1-4824-2946-6 (library binding)
 1. Titanic (Steamship)—Juvenile literature. 2. Shipwrecks—North Atlantic Ocean—Juvenile
literature. I. Title.

 G530.T6S43 2015
 910.9163'4—dc23

                              2015006046

First Edition

Published in 2016 by
Gareth Stevens Publishing
111 East 14th Street, Suite 349
New York, NY 10003

Copyright © 2016 Gareth Stevens Publishing

Designer: Katelyn E. Reynolds
Editor: Therese Shea

Photo credits: Cover, p. 1 OFF/AFP/Getty Images; cover, pp. 1–32 (background texture)
501room/Shutterstock.com; pp. 5, 7 Robert John Welch (1859-1936), official photographer
for Harland & Wolff/Wikipedia.org; pp. 9, 17, 23 (top) Hulton Archive/Getty Images;
pp. 10, 22 Universal Images Group/Getty Images; p. 11 Soerfm/Wikipedia.org; p. 13 (top)
New York Times/Wikipedia.org; p. 13 (bottom) Culture Club/Getty Images; p. 15 (main)
Topical Press Agency/Getty Images; pp. 15 (map), 20 Dorling Kindersley/Getty Images;
p. 16 The chief steward of the liner Prinz Adalbert/Wikipedia.org; p. 19 Peter Jackson/
The Bridgeman Art Library/Getty Images; p. 21 (top) Popperfoto/Getty Images; p. 21
(bottom) Bain News Service, publisher/Wikipedia.org; p. 23 (bottom) Library of Congress;
p. 27 Emory Kristof/National Geographic/Getty Images; p. 29 Courtesy of NOAA/Institute
for Exploration/University of Rhode Island (NOAA/IFE/URI)/Wikipedia.org.

Printed in the United States of America

CPSIA compliance information: Batch #CS15GS: For further information contact Gareth Stevens, New York, New York at 1-800-542-2595.

CONTENTS

Shore to Shore by Ship 4

Under Construction 6

"Practically Unsinkable" 8

Icy Warnings 12

"Iceberg, Right Ahead!" 14

The Unsinkable Sinks 18

Investigations 24

The *Titanic* Underwater 26

Legacy 28

Glossary 30

For More Information 31

Index 32

Words in the glossary appear in **bold** type
the first time they are used in the text.

SHORE TO SHORE BY SHIP

Imagine you had to travel to faraway places by ship. Before airplanes, that's just what people had to do. This wasn't a quick way to travel, but sometimes it was the only way. Naturally, travelers wanted ships that were both fast and comfortable.

In the early 1900s, two famous ship lines competed to construct the most popular vessels to transport passengers between Europe and the United States. These ship lines were called the Cunard Line and the White Star Line. In 1907, Cunard introduced the fastest passenger ships yet: the *Lusitania* and the *Mauretania*. In answer, White Star decided to build three luxury ships. One of these was the *Titanic*, the ship doomed to sink in the Atlantic just a few years later.

The Deadly Details

The *Lusitania* was sunk by a German **U-boat** on May 7, 1915. About 1,200 passengers died. This was one of the causes of the United States entering World War I (1914–1918).

Building a ship was a massive task. You can see how huge these ocean liners were in this photograph.

HARLAND AND WOLFF

The White Star Line didn't build its own ships. Instead, most were built by an Irish company called Harland and Wolff. The three luxury ships ordered for White Star were called the *Olympic*, the *Titanic*, and the *Britannic*. Construction on the *Olympic* was begun a few months before the *Titanic*. The two huge ships were built side by side and were called "sister ships" for their similarities. The *Olympic* was in service until 1935, unlike its ill-fated sister.

5

UNDER CONSTRUCTION

Construction of the *Titanic* began on March 31, 1909, at Harland and Wolff's shipyard in Belfast, Ireland. The ocean liner, designed by Thomas Andrews, was the height of luxury at that time. It had a first-class dining room, four elevators, a grand staircase, and a swimming pool. Its second-class rooms were much like first-class rooms on other ships, and its third-class offerings were noted for their comfort, too. There was also a library, a gym, a restaurant, a reading and writing room, and many other special areas and decks.

When construction was complete, the RMS *Titanic* was the largest passenger ship at the time. It measured 882 feet (269 m) in length and 92.5 feet (28 m) at its broadest point.

The Deadly Details

The *Titanic* had 29 giant boilers that powered its two main steam engines.

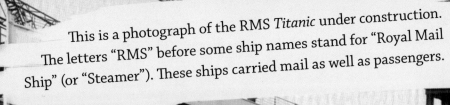

This is a photograph of the RMS *Titanic* under construction. The letters "RMS" before some ship names stand for "Royal Mail Ship" (or "Steamer"). These ships carried mail as well as passengers.

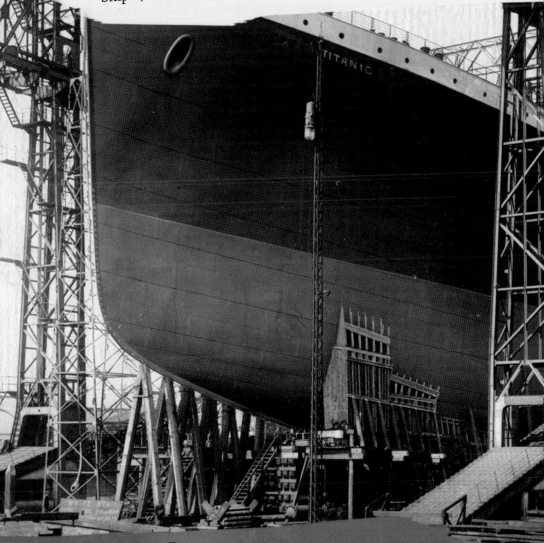

CLASSES

The *Titanic* had three classes of **accommodations**. First class was the most luxurious and expensive. Usually only very wealthy people could afford to sail first class. Second class was less costly. Third-class rooms were the least expensive, costing some about $20 to sail the Atlantic. There was space for about 700 third-class passengers, more than first-class and second-class combined. Third-class travel was how many liners made most of their profits, so it was worth it to make third-class rooms comfortable.

7

"PRACTICALLY UNSINKABLE"

The *Titanic* was built for safety, but unfortunately the safety designs had serious flaws. The ship had a double bottom and 16 **bulkheads** with watertight doors that could be opened from the **bridge**. *Shipbuilder* magazine called liners designed in this way "practically unsinkable." However, there was a problem: once water entered one of the compartments, it could spill into the next, and so on.

Also, lifeboat seats aboard the *Titanic* were fewer than the number of passengers. A total of 20 boats could carry 1,178 people. However, the ship could carry 2,435 passengers, and it needed a crew of about 900. Therefore, only about one-third of the total people aboard could claim a seat on a lifeboat.

The Deadly Details

The *Titanic*'s builders claimed that four compartments could be flooded without sinking the ship.

According to *National Geographic*, White Star and the British Board of Trade thought that too many lifeboats on deck would make people believe the ship was unsafe. You can see the boats on deck in this photograph taken before the disaster.

WHOSE FAULT?

The *Titanic* had room to carry 48 lifeboats, which might have saved everyone aboard its doomed voyage. But whose fault was the number of lifeboats? You could say that it was White Star's fault. They went to so much trouble making the ship luxurious, they could have made it extra safe, too. However, they probably thought they were. At that time, the *Titanic's* number of lifeboats exceeded the British Board of Trade's regulations.

The *Titanic*'s first launch was May 31, 1911. About 100,000 people watched. However, at that point, only its hull, or body, and main structure were complete. It was towed to another dock where thousands of workers finished its interior. In early April 1912, the ship underwent sea trials, or tests at sea. It was declared "seaworthy."

On April 10, 1912, the RMS *Titanic* was ready for its maiden, or first, voyage. It set sail from Southampton, England, and made stops in France and Ireland. On April 11 at 1:30 p.m., with 2,240 passengers, the *Titanic* set a course for New York City.

On board were wealthy businessmen and celebrities of the day, including millionaire John Jacob Astor IV; the owner of the store Macy's, Isidor Straus; and **industrialist** Benjamin Guggenheim.

The DEaDLy DEtaiLS

Also aboard the *Titanic* were the White Star Line's chairman, J. Bruce Ismay, and the ship's designer, Thomas Andrews.

The *Titanic*'s hull was the largest movable man-made object in 1911!

BAD START

The maiden voyage didn't start without trouble. A coal fire began in one of the *Titanic*'s storage containers. It didn't seem uncontrollable enough to stop the voyage though, so crew were ordered to fight it while the ship went to sea. As it was leaving the port of Southampton, the *Titanic* also nearly **collided** with another ship, the SS *New York*. Strangely, this crash so close to port, had it happened, might have saved the lives of *Titanic* passengers. Just 2 feet (61 cm) separated the *Titanic* and the *New York*!

11

ICY WARNINGS

The *Titanic* was equipped with radios so the crew could communicate with other ships. The radio operators received iceberg warnings for the route they were taking. However, for the most part, passengers experienced calm, clear seas.

On the night of April 14, the fourth day of the voyage, the ship entered an area known to have icebergs. Captain Edward Smith decided to take a course south, though the ship maintained its speed of 22 knots, or 25 miles (40 km) per hour.

At about 9:40 p.m., the ship *Mesaba* sent a warning of ice ahead to the radio operators. The message wasn't given to the *Titanic*'s bridge. At 10:55 p.m., the nearby ship *Californian* reported stopping because of surrounding ice.

The Deadly Details

The radio operator who took the message from the *Californian* was angry that the ship's report had interrupted him. He was busy sending messages for passengers.

Captain Edward Smith went to his room for the night about 9:20 p.m. on April 14.

UNLUCKY ICE?

Some people believe the *Titanic* was unlucky in choosing to sail in a year that had an unusually high number of icebergs in the North Atlantic Ocean. They say the moon's nearness to Earth on January 12, 1912, created a superhigh tide that set loose many icebergs 3 months before the *Titanic*'s collision. However, others say there are more icebergs today and an even greater chance of hitting one.

13

"ICEBERG, RIGHT AHEAD!"

The ship had a **crow's nest** in which crew could keep a lookout for danger. That night, Frederick Fleet and Reginald Lee were on duty. However, their **binoculars** were missing, making their job a bit more difficult. At about 11:40 p.m., when the ship was about 400 nautical miles (740 km) south of Newfoundland, Canada, Fleet cried, "Iceberg, right ahead!" He rang the warning bell and telephoned the bridge.

The crewman in charge, First Officer William Murdoch, quickly gave orders: reverse the engines and "hard-a-**starboard**" (turn to the left). It was too late. Ice pieces sprayed the decks. It seemed at first like they had avoided a collision, though. Captain Smith was called, and he and the ship's designer, Thomas Andrews, went below to inspect the damage.

The Deadly Details

Many think the *Titanic* wouldn't have been damaged as badly if the ship hadn't turned.

14

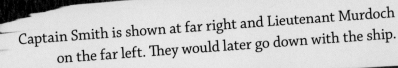
Captain Smith is shown at far right and Lieutenant Murdoch on the far left. They would later go down with the ship.

England
Ireland
France

New York City

ICEBLINK

Frederick Fleet reported **hazy** conditions that night that made spotting icebergs even harder. This may have been a condition called iceblink, in which light is reflected off an ice field causing a glow. The amount of ice researchers think was on the ocean that day meant conditions were perfect for iceblink. In fact, they wonder how the *Titanic* didn't hit an iceberg even sooner. By the time Fleet saw the iceberg, the ship was traveling too fast to avoid it.

What Smith and Andrews saw belowdecks horrified them. The ship's starboard side had scraped along the iceberg, causing a gash about 300 feet (91 m) long. At least five of the ship's "watertight" bulkheads were taking in water and quickly. Since these compartments were located at the bow, or front, of the ship, Andrews realized that part of the ship would begin to sink into the ocean. He believed the *Titanic* had about 90 more minutes afloat.

The radio operators were already calling for help from nearby ships. However, there was no telling when aid would arrive. It was clear it was time for evacuation. About an hour after the collision, the captain ordered people to begin filling the available lifeboats.

The DeadLy DetaiLS

The *Titanic*'s sister ship, the *Olympic*, heard the distress call, too. However, it was much too far away to help.

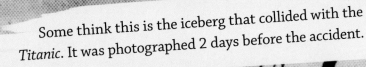
Some think this is the iceberg that collided with the *Titanic*. It was photographed 2 days before the accident.

SO CLOSE, YET SO FAR

There was a ship in sight of the *Titanic*, but the radio operators couldn't contact it. The *Californian*, the ship that had warned the *Titanic* of ice, was close but had turned off its radio for the night. The *Carpathia*, a Cunard ship, received a call for help about 12:20 a.m. and headed to assist the *Titanic*. However, it would take more than 3 hours to reach the quickly sinking vessel.

THE UNSINKABLE SINKS

The ship was taking on a lot of water very quickly, but above deck, it was hard to tell at first. Passengers couldn't get it out of their head that they were on an "unsinkable" vessel. They didn't believe it would go down. However, when the *Titanic* began to lean, panic set in.

The evacuation wasn't well planned. According to the law of the sea, women and children had to be loaded into the lifeboats first, before male passengers. Many women and children were trapped belowdecks and didn't even have a chance. Additionally, the lifeboats weren't completely filled in the disorder of the evacuation. Only 705 survivors were found in the boats when rescue came, although there was space for more than 1,100 in all.

The Deadly Details

Two of the nine dogs on board the ship were put into lifeboats.

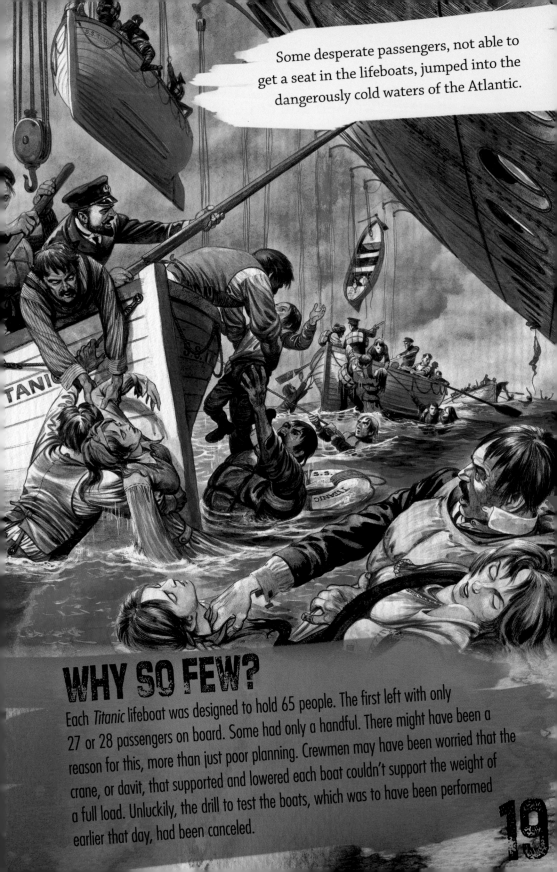

Some desperate passengers, not able to get a seat in the lifeboats, jumped into the dangerously cold waters of the Atlantic.

WHY SO FEW?

Each *Titanic* lifeboat was designed to hold 65 people. The first left with only 27 or 28 passengers on board. Some had only a handful. There might have been a reason for this, more than just poor planning. Crewmen may have been worried that the crane, or davit, that supported and lowered each boat couldn't support the weight of a full load. Unluckily, the drill to test the boats, which was to have been performed earlier that day, had been canceled.

Because women and children were loaded into the lifeboats first, some families were separated. Others refused to be, choosing to die together rather than live without each other. This was the case for Isador Straus and his wife Ida. They went back to their room to await their deaths together. Benjamin Guggenheim showed courage facing his fate, too. He changed into an evening suit and came back onto deck, supposedly saying: "We are dressed in our best and are prepared to go down like gentlemen."

The *Titanic*'s bow continued to sink more and more, causing its stern to rise out of the water. The ship broke in two about 2:18 a.m. The bow sank first, and then the stern went under at 2:20 a.m., plunging hundreds still on deck into the cold waters.

ThE DEaDLy DEtaiLS

Some men, usually elderly, did get on lifeboats. However, a few younger men, such as White Star chairman J. Bruce Ismay, were seen as cowards for doing so.

The *Titanic* was completely underwater only 3 hours after it hit the iceberg.

Margaret Brown

THE UNSINKABLE MOLLY BROWN

Margaret "Molly" Brown was an heiress who helped people remain calm while the lifeboats were loaded. She had to be forced to get into one of the last lifeboats. Brown went on to aid survivors, set up a fund for victims' families, and help construct the *Titanic* memorial in Washington, DC. She used her fame to promote women's causes, workers' rights, and education for children. The play and movie *The Unsinkable Molly Brown* is based on her story.

Once the ship went down, some lifeboat passengers refused to go back for the people who had fallen into the water. They worried that too many people would get in the boats and make them sink, too. Others, including Molly Brown, begged the people in their boat to go back to help. By the time the lifeboats finally turned around, almost everyone in the freezing waters had died, though. In all, about 1,500 lives were lost.

Finally, the *Carpathia* reached the lifeboats at about 3:30 a.m. It picked up the survivors and headed to New York City. Stories about the *Titanic* crowded newspapers. People demanded to know what had happened and why. Soon, investigations were underway in the United States and Great Britain.

The Deadly Details

The ocean waters in the North Atlantic that night were 28°F (−2°C), causing those in the water to develop **hypothermia**.

SILENT ALARM

A general alarm for all parts of the *Titanic* was never ordered or sounded. It's possible many third-class passengers didn't know to get on deck to be loaded onto the lifeboats. When they finally did, the boats were gone. Others may have been sleeping and become trapped belowdecks by the time they awoke. The majority of people who died aboard the *Titanic* were crewmen and third-class passengers.

INVESTIGATIONS

An American investigation of the *Titanic* sinking put the blame on the British Board of Trade for not having better regulations and inspections. It also blamed Captain Smith, who went down with the ship, for not slowing despite repeated ice warnings. Finally, it criticized the *Californian*, claiming the crew had ignored distress signals from the *Titanic*.

A British investigation was conducted by the British Board of Trade. The final report stated: "The loss of the said ship was due to collision with an iceberg, brought about by the excessive speed at which the ship was being navigated." However, the head judge of the investigation said the captain had acted as any other captain would have. This investigation, too, put some blame for the lives lost on the *Californian*.

The Deadly Details

Some people blame J. Bruce Ismay for the *Titanic*'s speed. They say he ordered the captain to break a speed record.

Timeline of the *Titanic* Tragedy

APRIL 10, 1912
- **9:30 a.m.** - Passengers begin boarding the RMS *Titanic* in Southampton, England.
- **noon** - The *Titanic* leaves the dock for its maiden voyage to France.
- **8:10 p.m.** - The *Titanic* leaves France for Ireland.

APRIL 11, 1912
- **1:30 p.m.** - The *Titanic* sets a course for New York City from Ireland.

APRIL 14, 1912
- **9:40 p.m.** - The *Mesaba* sends a warning of ice ahead.
- **10:55 p.m.** - The *Californian* reports stopping because of surrounding ice.
- **11:40 p.m.** - A lookout on the *Titanic* reports an iceberg ahead.

APRIL 15, 1912
- **12:20 a.m.** - The *Carpathia* receives a distress call from the *Titanic*.
- **2:18 a.m.** - The *Titanic* breaks in two. Its bow sinks.
- **2:20 a.m.** - The *Titanic*'s stern sinks.
- **3:30 a.m.** - The *Carpathia* reaches the *Titanic*'s lifeboats.

APRIL 18, 1912
- The *Carpathia* arrives in New York with 705 survivors.

UNFAIR OPINIONS?

The British investigation claimed the *Californian* "might have saved many, if not all, of the lives that were lost." Was that a fair assumption? The crew of the *Californian* claimed to be too far away to hear and see the distress signals. The American and British investigations believed the ship much closer. Some people think that the closer ship was actually a boat from Norway that was illegally hunting seals.

THE TITANIC UNDERWATER

The *Titanic* remained undisturbed on the ocean floor for decades. Explorers didn't have the **technology** needed to find it until later in the 20th century. On September 1, 1985, Robert Ballard and a research expedition plunged a **submersible** named *Argo* about 13,000 feet (4 km) into the North Atlantic. The *Argo*'s camera sent images of the ship to the researchers.

Many expeditions have visited the *Titanic* since then. Findings have produced both questions and answers. Many had expected to see huge holes in the ship from the collision with the iceberg. Instead, there were many thin gashes and cracks. The seams between hull plates had separated as well, making some wonder if low-quality steel or weak rivets were responsible for some of the damage.

The Deadly Details

The wreck is being eaten! Tiny organisms are consuming the iron.

The *Argo*, shown here, found the ship in two pieces on the ocean floor.

UNCOVERED ARTIFACTS

Many **artifacts** have been brought up from the *Titanic* that tell us about life and people back then. These include perfume bottles, shoes, decorations, passenger tickets, letters, jewelry, cameras, and more. Many museums house *Titanic* artifacts, including the Smithsonian in Washington, DC. Sometimes objects are sold, too. A violin that was played by the ship's bandleader to calm the passengers while it sank was sold for $1.7 million in 2013!

27

LEGACY

The *Titanic*'s sad fate had positive effects
on ocean travel in the years that followed.
In 1913, the first International Conference
for Safety of Life at Sea occurred in London,
England. Among the regulations decided upon
was that every ship had to have enough lifeboat
space for each person aboard. Another was that
all ships must have a 24-hour radio watch so that
they don't miss distress signals from other ships.

Though many had lost their lives already,
many more lives would be saved by these and
other regulations in years to come. The RMS
Titanic may have been
doomed to sink,
but ocean liners
would continue to
successfully cross
the Atlantic, never
forgetting the fate
of that ship one
cold April night.

The Deadly Details

After the *Titanic*'s sinking,
the International Ice Patrol
was formed to warn ships of
icebergs in the North Atlantic
and to break up ice.

The wreck is covered with "rusticles," or rusty icicles, which are actually communities of bacteria.

EXPLORING THE *TITANIC*

James Cameron, director of the 1997 movie *Titanic*, has made more than 30 dives to the wreck in all. His explorations helped him build the set of his movie. In 2012, he piloted the submersible *Mir 1* into the wreck and used a remote-controlled robot to explore its inner decks. Many of the windows, beds, and other fixtures are still intact. Some rooms look like they're untouched.

GLOSSARY

accommodation: a place where travelers can sleep and find other services

artifact: something made by people in the past

binoculars: a handheld visual tool composed of two telescopes and a focusing device

bridge: the forward part of a ship's structure from which the ship is navigated

bulkhead: a wall that separates the different parts of a ship or aircraft

collide: the hitting of two objects against one another

crow's nest: a platform with short walls that is high on a ship from which you can see things that are far away

hazy: partly hidden, darkened, or clouded by dust, smoke, or mist

hypothermia: dangerously low body temperature caused by cold conditions

industrialist: someone who owns or manages an industry

starboard: the side of a ship that is on the right when you are looking toward the front

submersible: a small vehicle that operates underwater and is used especially for research

technology: the way people do something using tools and the tools that they use

U-boat: a German submarine used during World Wars I and II

FOR MORE INFORMATION

BOOKS

Callery, Sean. *Titanic*. New York, NY: Scholastic, 2014.

Stewart, David. *You Wouldn't Want to Sail on the Titanic! One Voyage You'd Rather Not Make*. New York, NY: Franklin Watts, 2013.

Stewart, Melissa. *Titanic*. Washington, DC: National Geographic, 2012.

WEBSITES

The Titanic
ngm.nationalgeographic.com/2012/04/titanic/cameron-text
Read about James Cameron's "ghostwalk" through the ship.

Titanic: Sinking the Myths
www.bbc.co.uk/history/british/britain_wwone/titanic_01.shtml
Read more about the people and events aboard the *Titanic*.

INDEX

Andrews, Thomas 6, 10, 14, 16

Argo 26, 27

artifacts 27

Ballard, Robert 26

Britannic 5

British Board of Trade 9, 24

Brown, Molly 21, 22

Californian 12, 17, 24, 25

Cameron, James 29

Carpathia 17, 22, 23, 25

Cunard Line 4, 17

evacuation 16, 18

Fleet, Frederick 14, 15

Guggenheim, Benjamin 10, 20

Harland and Wolff 5, 6

icebergs 12, 13, 14, 15, 16, 17, 21, 24, 25, 26, 28

iceblink 15

International Conference for Safety of Life at Sea 28

International Ice Patrol 28

investigations 22, 24, 25

Ismay, J. Bruce, 10, 20, 24

Lee, Reginald 14

lifeboats 8, 9, 16, 18, 19, 20, 21, 22, 23, 25, 28

Lusitania 4

maiden voyage 10, 11, 25

Mesaba 12, 25

Mir I 29

Murdoch, William 14, 15

Olympic 5, 16

radio 12, 16, 17, 28

Smith, Edward 12, 13, 14, 15, 16, 24

Southampton, England 10, 11, 25

Straus, Isador 10, 20

survivors 18, 21, 22, 25

White Star Line 4, 5, 9

women and children 18, 20